D1551347

RIDERS TO THE SEA

By

J. M. SYNGE

JOHN W. LUCE & COMPANY
BOSTON : : : : : : : 1911

INTRODUCTION

It must have been on Synge's second visit to
the Aran Islands that he had the experience
out of which was wrought what many believe
to be his greatest play. The scene of "Riders
to the Sea" is laid in a cottage on Inishmaan,
the middle and most interesting island of the
Aran group. While Synge was on Inishmaan,
the story came to him of a man whose body
had been washed up on the far away coast of
Donegal, and who, by reason of certain pecu-
liarities of dress, was suspected to be from the
island. In due course, he was recognised as
a native of Inishmaan, in exactly the manner
described in the play, and perhaps one of the
most poignantly vivid passages in Synge's book
on "The Aran Islands" relates the incident of
his burial.

The other element in the story which Synge
introduces into the play is equally true. Many
tales of "second sight" are to be heard among
Celtic races. In fact, they are so common as

to arouse little or no wonder in the minds of the people. It is just such a tale, which there seems no valid reason for doubting, that Synge heard, and that gave the title, "Riders to the Sea", to his play.

It is the dramatist's high distinction that he has simply taken the materials which lay ready to his hand, and by the power of sympathy woven them, with little modification, into a tragedy which, for dramatic irony and noble pity, has no equal among its contemporaries.

Great tragedy, it is frequently claimed with some show of justice, has perforce departed with the advance of modern life and its complicated tangle of interests and creature comforts. A highly developed civilisation, with its attendant specialisation of culture, tends ever to lose sight of those elemental forces, those primal emotions, naked to wind and sky, which are the stuff from which great drama is wrought by the artist, but which, as it would seem, are rapidly departing from us.

It is only in the far places, where solitary communion may be had with the elements, that this dynamic life is still to be found continuously, and it is accordingly thither that the dramatist, who would deal with spiritual life disengaged from the environment of an intellectual maze, must go for that experience which will beget in him inspiration for his art.

The Aran Islands from which Synge gained his inspiration are rapidly losing that sense of isolation and self-dependence, which has hitherto been their rare distinction, and which furnished the motivation for Synge's masterpiece. Whether or not Synge finds a successor, it is none the less true that in English dramatic literature "Riders to the Sea" has an historic value which it would be difficult to overestimate in its accomplishment and its possibilities. A writer in The Manchester Guardian shortly after Synge's death phrased it rightly when he wrote that it is "the tragic masterpiece of our language in our time; wherever it has been played in Europe from Galway to Prague, it has made the word tragedy mean something more profoundly stirring and cleansing to the spirit than it did."

The secret of the play's power is its capacity for standing afar off, and mingling, if we may say so, sympathy with relentlessness. There is a wonderful beauty of speech in the words of every character, wherein the latent power of suggestion is almost unlimited. "In the big world the old people do be leaving things after them for their sons and children, but in this place it is the young men do be leaving things behind for them that do be old." In the quavering rhythm of these words, there is poignantly present that quality of strangeness and remoteness in beauty which, as we are coming to realise, is the touchstone of Celtic literary art. However, the very asceticism of the play has begotten a corresponding power which lifts Synge's work far out of the current of the Irish literary revival, and sets it high in a timeless atmosphere of universal action.

Its characters live — and die. It is their virtue in life to be lonely, and none but the lonely man in tragedy may be great. He dies, and then it is the virtue in life of the women — mothers and wives and sisters — to be great in their loneliness, great as Maurya, the stricken mother, is great in her final word.

" Michael has a clean burial in the far north, by the grace of the Almighty God. Bartley will have a fine coffin out of the white boards, and a deep grave surely. What more can we want than that? No man at all can be living for ever, and we must be satisfied."

The pity and the terror of it all have brought a great peace, the peace that passeth understanding, and it is because the play holds this timeless peace after the storm which has bowed down every character, that " Riders to the Sea " may rightly take its place as the greatest modern tragedy in the English tongue.

EDWARD J. O'BRIEN.

February 23, 1911.

RIDERS TO THE SEA

RIDERS TO THE SEA

A Play in One Act

*First performed at the Molesworth Hall,
Dublin, February 25th, 1904.*

PERSONS

MAURYA (*an old woman*) . Honor Lavelle

BARTLEY (*her son*) . . . W. G. Fay

CATHLEEN (*her daughter*) Sarah Allgood

NORA (*a younger daughter*) Emma Vernon

MEN AND WOMEN

RIDERS TO THE SEA

A Play in One Act

First performed at the Molesworth Hall, Dublin, February 25th, 1904.

Scene.— *An Island off the West of Ireland.*

(Cottage kitchen, with nets, oil-skins, spinning wheel, some new boards standing by the wall, etc. Cathleen, a girl of about twenty, finishes kneading cake, and puts it down in the pot-oven by the fire; then wipes her hands, and begins to spin at the wheel. Nora, a young girl, puts her head in at the door.)

NORA

In a low voice.

Where is she?

CATHLEEN

She's lying down, God help her, and may be sleeping, if she's able.

17

*Nora comes in softly, and takes a
bundle from under her shawl.*

CATHLEEN

Spinning the wheel rapidly.

What is it you have?

NORA

The young priest is after bringing them.
It's a shirt and a plain stocking were got off
a drowned man in Donegal.

*Cathleen stops her wheel with a
sudden movement, and leans out to
listen.*

NORA

We're to find out if it's Michael's they are,
some time herself will be down looking by the
sea.

CATHLEEN

How would they be Michael's, Nora. How
would he go the length of that way to the far
north?

NORA

The young priest says he's known the like
of it. " If it's Michael's they are," says he,
" you can tell herself he's got a clean burial
by the grace of God, and if they're not his,

18

let no one say a word about them, for she'll
be getting her death," says he, " with crying
and lamenting."

*The door which Nora half closed is
blown open by a gust of wind.*

CATHLEEN

Looking out anxiously.

Did you ask him would he stop Bartley
going this day with the horses to the Galway
fair?

NORA

" I won't stop him," says he, " but let you
not be afraid. Herself does be saying prayers
half through the night, and the Almighty God
won't leave her destitute," says he, " with no
son living."

CATHLEEN

Is the sea bad by the white rocks, Nora?

NORA

Middling bad, God help us. There's a great
roaring in the west, and it's worse it'll be
getting when the tide's turned to the wind.

*She goes over to the table with the
bundle.*

Shall I open it now?

19

CATHLEEN

Maybe she'd wake up on us, and come in before we'd done.

Coming to the table.

It's a long time we'll be, and the two of us crying.

NORA

Goes to the inner door and listens.

She's moving about on the bed. She'll be coming in a minute.

CATHLEEN

Give me the ladder, and I'll put them up in the turf-loft, the way she won't know of them at all, and maybe when the tide turns she'll be going down to see would he be floating from the east.

> *They put the ladder against the gable of the chimney; Cathleen goes up a few steps and hides the bundle in the turf-loft. Maurya comes from the inner room.*

MAURYA

Looking up at Cathleen and speaking querulously.

Isn't it turf enough you have for this day and evening?

CATHLEEN

There's a cake baking at the fire for a short space

Throwing down the turf

and Bartley will want it when the tide turns if he goes to Connemara.

Nora picks up the turf and puts it round the pot-oven.

MAURYA

Sitting down on a stool at the fire.

He won't go this day with the wind rising from the south and west. He won't go this day, for the young priest will stop him surely.

NORA

He'll not stop him, mother, and I heard Eamon Simon and Stephen Pheety and Colum Shawn saying he would go.

MAURYA

Where is he itself?

NORA

He went down to see would there be another

boat sailing in the week, and I'm thinking it won't be long till he's here now, for the tide's turning at the green head, and the hooker's tacking from the east.

CATHLEEN

I hear some one passing the big stones.

NORA

Looking out.

He's coming now, and he in a hurry.

BARTLEY

Comes in and looks round the room.
Speaking sadly and quietly.

Where is the bit of new rope, Cathleen, was bought in Connemara?

CATHLEEN

Coming down.

Give it to him, Nora; it's on a nail by the white boards. I hung it up this morning, for the pig with the black feet was eating it.

NORA

Giving him a rope.
Is that it, Bartley?

MAURYA

You'd do right to leave that rope, Bartley,

hanging by the boards (*Bartley takes the rope*). It will be wanting in this place, I'm telling you, if Michael is washed up to-morrow morning, or the next morning, or any morning in the week, for it's a deep grave we'll make him by the grace of God.

BARTLEY

Beginning to work with the rope.

I've no halter the way I can ride down on the mare, and I must go now quickly. This is the one boat going for two weeks or beyond it, and the fair will be a good fair for horses I heard them saying below.

MAURYA

It's a hard thing they'll be saying below if the body is washed up and there's no man in it to make the coffin, and I after giving a big price for the finest white boards you'd find in Connemara.

She looks round at the boards.

BARTLEY

How would it be washed up, and we after looking each day for nine days, and a strong wind blowing a while back from the west and south?

MAURYA

If it wasn't found itself, that wind **is** raising the sea, and there was a star up against the moon, and it rising in the night. If it was a hundred horses, or a thousand horses you had itself, what is the price of a thousand horses against a son where there is one son only?

BARTLEY

Working at the halter, to Cathleen.

Let you go down each day, and see the sheep aren't jumping in on the rye, and if the jobber comes you can sell the pig with the black feet if there is a good price going.

MAURYA

How would the like of her get a good price for a pig?

BARTLEY

To Cathleen.

If the west wind holds with the last bit of the moon let you and Nora get up weed enough for another cock for the kelp. It's hard set we'll be from this day with no one in it but one man to work.

MAURYA

It's hard set we'll be surely the day you're

drownd'd with the rest. What way will I live and the girls with me, and I an old woman looking for the grave?

Bartley lays down the halter, takes off his old coat, and puts on a newer one of the same flannel.

BARTLEY

To Nora.

Is she coming to the pier?

NORA

Looking out.

She's passing the green head and letting fall her sails.

BARTLEY

Getting his purse and tobacco.

I'll have half an hour to go down, and you'll see me coming again in two days, or in three days, or maybe in four days if the wind is bad.

MAURYA

Turning round to the fire, and puting her shawl over her head.

Isn't it a hard and cruel man won't hear a word from an old woman, and she holding him from the sea?

CATHLEEN

It's the life of a young man to be going on the sea, and who would listen to an old woman with one thing and she saying it over?

BARTLEY

Taking the halter.

I must go now quickly. I'll ride down on the red mare, and the gray pony 'll run behind me. . . The blessing of God on you.

He goes out.

MAURYA

Crying out as he is in the door.

He's gone now, God spare us, and we'll not see him again. He's gone now, and when the black night is falling I'll have no son left me in the world.

CATHLEEN

Why wouldn't you give him your blessing and he looking round in the door? Isn't it sorrow enough is on every one in this house without your sending him out with an unlucky word behind him, and a hard word in his ear?

Maurya takes up the tongs and begins raking the fire aimlessly without looking round.

26

NORA

Turning towards her.

You're taking away the turf from the cake.

CATHLEEN

Crying out.

The Son of God forgive us, Nora, we're after forgetting his bit of bread.

She comes over to the fire.

NORA

And it's destroyed he'll be going till dark night, and he after eating nothing since the sun went up.

CATHLEEN

Turning the cake out of the oven.

It's destroyed he'll be, surely. There's no sense left on any person in a house where an old woman will be talking for ever.

Maurya sways herself on her stool.

CATHLEEN

Cutting off some of the bread and rolling it in a cloth; to Maurya.

Let you go down now to the spring well and give him this and he passing. You'll see him then and the dark word will be broken, and you can say " God speed you," the way he'll be easy in his mind.

MAURYA

Taking the bread.

Will I be in it as soon as himself?

CATHLEEN

If you go now quickly.

MAURYA

Standing up unsteadily.

It's hard set I am to walk.

CATHLEEN

Looking at her anxiously.

Give her the stick, Nora, or maybe she'll slip on the big stones.

NORA

What stick?

CATHLEEN

The stick Michael brought from Connemara.

MAURYA

Taking a stick Nora gives her.

In the big world the old people do be leaving things after them for their sons and

28

children, but in this place it is the young men
do be leaving things behind for them that do
be old.

She goes out slowly.
Nora goes over to the ladder.

CATHLEEN

Wait, Nora, maybe she'd turn back quickly.
She's that sorry, God help her, you wouldn't
know the thing she'd do.

NORA

Is she gone round by the bush?

CATHLEEN

Looking out.

She's gone now. Throw it down quickly,
for the Lord knows when she'll be out of it
again.

NORA

Getting the bundle from the loft.

The young priest said he'd be passing to-
morrow, and we might go down and speak
to him below if it's Michael's they are surely.

CATHLEEN

Taking the bundle.
Did he say what way they were found?

NORA

Coming down.

" There were two men," says he, " and they rowing round with poteen before the cocks crowed, and the oar of one of them caught the body, and they passing the black cliffs of the north."

CATHLEEN

Trying to open the bundle.

Give me a knife, Nora, the string's perished with the salt water, and there's a black knot on it you wouldn't loosen in a week.

NORA

Giving her a knife.

I've heard tell it was a long way to Donegal.

CATHLEEN

Cutting the string.

It is surely. There was a man in here a while ago — the man sold us that knife — and he said if you set off walking from the rocks beyond, it would be seven days you'd be in Donegal.

NORA

And what time would a man take, and he floating?

*Cathleen opens the bundle and takes
out a bit of a stocking. They look
at them eagerly.*

CATHLEEN

In a low voice.

The Lord spare us, Nora! isn't it a queer
hard thing to say if it's his they are surely?

NORA

I'll get his shirt off the hook the way we
can put the one flannel on the other (*she
looks through some clothes hanging in the
corner.*) It's not with them, Cathleen, and
where will it be?

CATHLEEN

I'm thinking Bartley put it on him in the
morning, for his own shirt was heavy with
the salt in it (*pointing to the corner*). There's
a bit of a sleeve was of the same stuff. Give
me that and it will do.

*Nora brings it to her and they com-
pare the flannel.*

CATHLEEN

It's the same stuff, Nora; but if it is itself
aren't there great rolls of it in the shops of
Galway, and isn't it many another man may
have a shirt of it as well as Michael himself?

NORA

*Who has taken up the stocking and
counted the stitches, crying out.*

It's Michael, Cathleen, it's Michael; God
spare his soul, and what will herself say when
she hears this story, and Bartley on the sea?

CATHLEEN

Taking the stocking.

It's a plain stocking.

NORA

It's the second one of the third pair I
knitted, and I put up three score stitches, and
I dropped four of them.

CATHLEEN

Counts the stitches.

It's that number is in it (*crying out.*)
Ah, Nora, isn't it a bitter thing to think of
him floating that way to the far north, and
no one to keen him but the black hags that do
be flying on the sea?

NORA

*Swinging herself round, and throw-
ing out her arms on the clothes.*

And isn't it a pitiful thing when there is

nothing left of a man who was a great rower
and fisher, but a bit of an old shirt and a plain
stocking?

CATHLEEN

After an instant.

Tell me is herself coming, Nora? I hear
a little sound on the path.

NORA

Looking out.

She is, Cathleen. She's coming up to the
door.

CATHLEEN

Put these things away before she'll come
in. Maybe it's easier she'll be after giving
her blessing to Bartley, and we won't let on
we've heard anything the time he's on the sea.

NORA

Helping Cathleen to close the bundle.

We'll put them here in the corner.

*They put them into a hole in the
chimney corner. Cathleen goes back
to the spinning-wheel.*

NORA

Will she see it was crying I was?

CATHLEEN

Keep your back to the door the way the light'll not be on you.

Nora sits down at the chimney corner, with her back to the door. Maurya comes in very slowly, without looking at the girls, and goes over to her stool at the other side of of the fire. The cloth with the bread is still in her hand. The girls look at each other, and Nora points to the bundle of bread.

CATHLEEN

After spinning for a moment.

You didn't give him his bit of bread?

Maurya begins to keen softly, without turning round.

CATHLEEN

Did you see him riding down?

Maurya goes on keening.

CATHLEEN

A little impatiently.

God forgive you; isn't it a better thing to raise your voice and tell what you seen, than to be making lamentation for a thing that's done? Did you see Bartley, I'm saying to you.

MAURYA

With a weak voice.

My heart's broken from this day.

CATHLEEN

As before.

Did you see Bartley?

MAURYA

I seen the fearfulest thing.

CATHLEEN

Leaves her wheel and looks out.

God forgive you; he's riding the mare now over the green head, and the gray pony behind him.

MAURYA

Starts, so that her shawl falls back from her head and shows her white tossed hair. With a frightened voice.

The gray pony behind him.

CATHLEEN

Coming to the fire.

What is it ails you, at all?

MAURYA

Speaking very slowly.

I've seen the fearfulest thing any person has seen, since the day Bride Dara seen the dead man with the child in his arms.

CATHLEEN AND NORA

Uah.

> *They crouch down in front of the old woman at the fire.*

NORA

Tell us what it is you seen.

MAURYA

I went down to the spring well, and I stood there saying a prayer to myself. Then Bartley came along, and he riding on the red mare with the gray pony behind him (*she puts up her hands, as if to hide something from her eyes.*) The Son of God spare us, Nora!

CATHLEEN

What is it you seen.

MAURYA

I seen Michael himself.

CATHLEEN

Speaking softly.

36

You did not, mother; It wasn't Michael you seen, for his body is after being found in the far north, and he's got a clean burial by the grace of God.

MAURYA

A little defiantly.

I'm after seeing him this day, and he riding and galloping. Bartley came first on the red mare; and I tried to say " God speed you," but something choked the words in my throat. He went by quickly; and " the blessing of God on you," says he, and I could say nothing. I looked up then, and I crying, at the gray pony, and there was Michael upon it — with fine clothes on him, and new shoes on his feet.

CATHLEEN

Begins to keen.

It's destroyed we are from this day. It's destroyed, surely.

NORA

Didn't the young priest say the Almighty God wouldn't leave her destitute with no son living?

MAURYA

In a low voice, but clearly.

It's little the like of him knows of the sea.
. . . Bartley will be lost now, and let
you call in Eamon and make me a good coffin
out of the white boards, for I won't live after
them. I've had a husband, and a husband's
father, and six sons in this house — six fine
men, though it was a hard birth I had with
every one of them and they coming to the
world — and some of them were found and
some of them were not found, but they're
gone now the lot of them. . . There were
Stephen, and Shawn, were lost in the great
wind, and found after in the Bay of Gregory
of the Golden Mouth, and carried up the two
of them on the one plank, and in by that door.

*She pauses for a moment, the girls
start as if they heard something
through the door that is half open
behind them.*

NORA

In a whisper.

Did you hear that, Cathleen? Did you hear
a noise in the north-east?

CATHLEEN

In a whisper.

There's some one after crying out by the
seashore.

MAURYA

Continues without hearing anything.

There was Sheamus and his father, and his own father again, were lost in a dark night, and not a stick or sign was seen of them when the sun went up. There was Patch after was drowned out of a curagh that turned over. I was sitting here with Bartley, and he a baby, lying on my two knees, and I seen two women, and three women, and four women coming in, and they crossing themselves, and not saying a word. I looked out then, and there were men coming after them, and they holding a thing in the half of a red sail, and water dripping out of it — it was a dry day, Nora — and leaving a track to the door.

> *She pauses again with her hand stretched out towards the door. It opens softly and old women begin to come in, crossing themselves on the threshold, and kneeling down in front of the stage with red petticoats over their heads.*

MAURYA

Half in a dream, to Cathleen.

Is it Patch, or Michael, or what is it at all?

CATHLEEN

Michael is after being found in the far north, and when he is found there how could he be here in this place?

MAURYA

There does be a power of young men floating round in the sea, and what way would they know if it was Michael they had, or another man like him, for when a man is nine days in the sea, and the wind blowing, it's hard set his own mother would be to say what man was it.

CATHLEEN

It's Michael, God spare him, for they're after sending us a bit of his clothes from the far north.

She reaches out and hands Maurya the clothes that belonged to Michael. Maurya stands up slowly, and takes them in her hands. Nora looks out.

NORA

They're carrying a thing among them and there's water dripping out of it and leaving a track by the big stones.

CATHLEEN

*In a whisper to the women who
have come in.*

Is it Bartley it is?

ONE OF THE WOMEN

It is surely, God rest his soul.
*Two younger women come in and
pull out the table. Then men carry
in the body of Bartley, laid on a
plank, with a bit of a sail over it,
and lay it on the table.*

CATHLEEN

To the women, as they are doing so.
What way was he drowned?

ONE OF THE WOMEN

The gray pony knocked him into the sea,
and he was washed out where there is a
great surf on the white rocks.

*Maurya has gone over and knelt
down at the head of the table. The
women are keening softly and sway-
ing themselves with a slow movement. Cathleen and Nora kneel at
the other end of the table. The men
kneel near the door.*

41

MAURYA

*Raising her head and speaking as if
she did not see the people around her.*

They're all gone now, and there isn't anything more the sea can do to me. . . . I'll
have no call now to be up crying and praying
when the wind breaks from the south, and
you can hear the surf is in the east, and the
surf is in the west, making a great stir with
the two noises, and they hitting one on the
other. I'll have no call now to be going down
and getting Holy Water in the dark nights
after Samhain, and I won't care what way
the sea is when the other women will be
keening. (*To Nora*). Give me the Holy
Water, Nora, there's a small sup still on the
dresser.

Nora gives it to her.

MAURYA

*Drops Michael's clothes across Bart-
ley's feet, and sprinkles the Holy
Water over him.*

It isn't that I haven't prayed for you,
Bartley, to the Almighty God. It isn't that
I haven't said prayers in the dark night till
you wouldn't know what I'ld be saying; but
it's a great rest I'll have now, and it's

time surely. It's a great rest I'll have now, and great sleeping in the long nights after Samhain, if it's only a bit of wet flour we do have to eat, and maybe a fish that would be stinking.

She kneels down again, crossing herself, and saying prayers under her breath.

CATHLEEN

To an old man.

Maybe yourself and Eamon would make a coffin when the sun rises. We have fine white boards herself bought, God help her, thinking Michael would be found, and I have a new cake you can eat while you'll be working.

THE OLD MAN

Looking at the boards.

Are there nails with them?

CATHLEEN

There are not, Colum; we didn't think of the nails.

ANOTHER MAN

It's a great wonder she wouldn't think of the nails, and all the coffins she's seen made already.

CATHLEEN

It's getting old she is, and broken.

Maurya stands up again very slowly and spreads out the pieces of Michael's clothes beside the body, sprinkling them with the last of the Holy Water.

NORA

In a whisper to Cathleen.

She's quiet now and easy; but the day Michael was drowned you could hear her crying out from this to the spring well. It's fonder she was of Michael, and would any one have thought that?

CATHLEEN

Slowly and clearly.

An old woman will be soon tired with anything she will do, and isn't it nine days herself is after crying and keening, and making great sorrow in the house?

MAURYA

Puts the empty cup mouth downwards on the table, and lays her hands together on Bartley's feet.

They're all together this time, and the end

44

is come. May the Almighty God have mercy on Bartley's soul, and on Michael's soul, and on the souls of Sheamus and Patch, and Stephen and Shawn (*bending her head*); and may He have mercy on my soul, Nora, and on the soul of every one is left living in the world.

> *She pauses, and the keen rises a little more loudly from the women, then sinks away.*

MAURYA

Continuing.

Michael has a clean burial in the far north, by the grace of the Almighty God. Bartley will have a fine coffin out of the white boards, and a deep grave surely. What more can we want than that? No man at all can be living for ever, and we must be satisfied.

> *She kneels down again and the curtain falls slowly.*